I0541248

THE AMERICAN CARS
COLORING BOOK

CREATED BY BILL OWENS

ILLUSTRATIONS BY FRANCESCA COSANTI
ESSAY BY GEIR JORDAHL
DESIGN BY KATE JORDAHL

JACK KEROUAC
ALBERT SAIJO
LEW WELCH

TRIP TRAP

**Haiku along the Road from
San Francisco to New York • 1959**

A 1949, four-cylinder **"Hurricane"**
Willies Jeep Wagon was featured
on the cover of the first edition of
the 1975 Jack Kerouac book *TRIP
TRAP*.

Bill Owens - Founder of the Buffalo Bills Brewery and the American Distilling Institute; Author of multiple photography books, including *Suburbia* and the dystopian novel, *The Delco Years*

A NATION OF TURTLES - AN INTRODUCTION

Cars are an integral part of all of life's defining moments and experiences – vacations, relationships, jobs, families, successes and failures – our dreams fulfilled. The car is always there. The car defines us as Americans. It is our second home. It is the embodiment of freedom – our modern-day chariot.

We are, as Bill Owens calls us, "a nation of turtles." With our homes on our backs, we wander, we travel, we commute, we explore. Bill Owens' photographs invite us to reminisce about our cars past and present that shape our story.

My family's first automobile after arriving in America was a 1950 Buick. What I recall most about that car was its wonderful smell – a mix of stale oil, off-gassing upholstery, and other mysterious fumes and fragrances. These aromas, and the jerking back and forth as gears shifted, shaped my memories of life as an immigrant in a new country.

I got my first car at the age of sixteen. It was a 1964 Buick Wildcat. My Buick initiated me into a new world of freedom. For $140, I had four wheels and

for twenty-three cents, I could take those wheels nine miles down the road to school, to work, and, best of all, on a date.

Bill Owens' photographs and Francesca Cosanti's illustrations show us the car as an object, the car as a dream, the car as identity, and, ultimately, the car itself as a work of art.

Bill's pictures made in the mid 1970's embody a prescient sense of nostalgia and romanticism. They were ahead of their time.

Within the photographs and now illustrations, the cars become timeless. Bill Owen's saw all cars – the newest, the oldest, the common, the grand, and the absurd – in the light of our hopes and dreams.

Like a first car, like a first love, all his cars are idealized, yet tinged with a hint of loss.

Geir Jordahl

Essay adapted from Bill Owens CARS: A Completely American Reality, Copyright 2021, True North Editions.

THE CARS

The **Ford Mustang** was the dream of the 1960s baby boomers. With 22,000 pre-orders, it was the most successful car ever launched.

FORD MUSTANG

The 1953 **Buick Roadmaster Estate Wagon** had a carpeted rear platform that stretched 6 feet from to back and 5 feet from side to side. It could carry six people and all their luggage. It was the perfect car for large family travel.

BUICK ROADMASTER

The **Hudson Commodore** was produced between 1941 and 1952. It had a step-down mono-built body, making it lower than other contemporary cars. The interior was designed by Betty Thatcher, the first woman designer employed by a car manufacturer.

HUDSON COMMODORE

The 1949 **Cadillac Coupe Deville**, with 160 horsepower, was the first Cadillac to do 100 mph.

CADILLAC COUPE DEVILLE

The 1957 **Hudson Hornet** was
the last year of production for the
brand, it was very popular with
stock car racers but after the
brand was absorbed by AMC they
banned it from racing.

HUDSON HORNET

1957 **Buick LeSabre Convertible**.
Only 53,000 LeSabre Convertibles
were produced. It was available with
a 455 V8 motor.

BUICK LESABRE CONVERTIBLE

The **Chevrolet 150** was an economy car. It came with a six-cylinder 235 cubic inch inline engine. It was the classic family car.

CHEVROLET 150

The 1953 **Studebaker Commander Deluxe.** It came with a 232 cubic inch OHV V8 producing 120 horsepower. Known for its performance and fuel economy, this car with an automatic transmission made it an ideal touring car.

STUDEBAKER COMMANDER DELUXE

Chrysler Town and Country Woody was manufactured in Detroit and then Los Angeles. Only 3,309 Chrysler Town and County were built. It had a flathead straight eight and a fluid drive transmission. The Honduran Mahogany Wooden panels were later replaced with vinyl.

CHRYSLER TOWN & COUNTRY WOODY

1956 **Ford Thunderbird Hardtop Convertible.** The spare tire "Continental kit" was mounted on the bumper to free up trunk space. The exhaust pipes also came through the bumper.

FORD THUNDERBIRD HARDTOP CONVERTIBLE

1964 **Valiant Wagon.** The Valiant Wagon had a slant six engine, and the interior was made of very durable fabrics and materials to withstand family use.

VALIANT WAGON

1957 **Lincoln Premier** was known for its stylish exterior and high-end interior and features. It had a very poor fuel economy at 8 miles per gallon, and today nobody could afford to drive this car.

LINCOLN PREMIER

The **Chrysler Windsor Coupe** was a solid choice for 1946, providing ample power to cruise America's highways.

CHRYSLER WINDSOR COUPE

1957 **Plymouth Fury** gained fame for being the villain in the best selling Stephen King novel *Christine*.

PLYMOUTH FURY

1957 **Studebaker Golden Hawk**
was a pillarless Luxury Hardtop
with a 275 horsepwer motor. There
were only 51 cars made, making it a
rare collector's automobile. Only a
handful are known to have survived.

STUDEBAKER GOLDEN HAWK

The 1959 **Buick Electra 225 Convertible** was a luxury car with a long, low profile and luxurious interior. The Buick had a 401 cubic inch Wildcat engine that produced 325 horsepower.

BUICK ELECTRA 225 CONVERTIBLE

The **Plymouth Road Runner Superbird** was designed by Plymouth to lure Richard Petty to their stock car team. Its horn made a unique Beep-beep sound like the Roadrunner cartoon character, hence the moniker. There are less than 1000 examples of this car left in the world.

PLYMOUTH ROAD RUNNER SUPERBIRD

1959 **Nash Metropolitan.** Only 1,947 were produced. Nicknamed the Baby Nash, it was available in hardtop and convertible. You had to access the trunk through the backseat.

NASH METROPOLITAN

The **Studebaker Avanti Coupe** was
in production in 1962 and 1963, and
under 6000 cars were produced.

STUDEBAKER AVANTI COUPE

The 1970 **AMC AMX** was a two-seater sports car designed to compete with Corvette. It had a 325 horsepower V8 engine. Only 4,116 were produced.

AMC AMX

1956 **Desoto Firedome** was a mid-century design that was bold and advanced for its time. It had a Hemi V8 engine that produced 230 horsepower. It was one of the first cars produced with a high-compression V8 engine.

DESOTO FIREDOME

The 1970 **Chevrolet El Camino SS** came with a number of engine options. The most powerful was the 454. It could go from 0 to 60 in just under 7 seconds and had a top speed of 120 mph.

CHEVROLET EL CAMINO SS

The 1964 **Studebaker Daytona** is a
rare car with only 2,414 produced.

STUDEBAKER DAYTONA

The 1974 **Corvette Stingray** had a 454 cubic inch big block motor producing 270 horsepower. It had an optional luggage rack mounted on the trunk. It also came with lap and shoulder harness seatbelts that weren't readily available at the time.

CORVETTE STINGRAY

The 1958 **Edsel Pacer** had many innovative ideas, including a floating speedometer that glowed once it passed a pre-set speed limit.

EDSEL PACER

The **Pontiac Firebird Trans Am's** standard engine was a 400 cubic inch V8 motor producing 185 horsepower. There was also a 455 V8 with 200 horsepower. This was not available in California due to strict state emissions regulations.

PONTIAC FIREBIRD TRANS AM

My Neighbor Jim with his 1931
Chevy Rat Rod. Jim owns 18 cars.
A few of them are classics.

CHEVY RAT ROD

Bill Owens was born in 1938 in San Jose California. From his travels as far afield as India and including a Peace Corps tour in Jamaica, he developed his unique skills and aptitude as an anthropological and social photographer. His book, *Suburbia,* one of the 100 seminal books of the 20th century, captured the change in his home territory with much the same spirit of the traveler that he brought to foreign places. *Our Kind of People* (1975), *Working* (1977 and *Leisure* (1979), followed *Suburbia.* Bill Owens' work is in museums and collections throughout the world.. He has received a Guggenheim Fellowship and two NEA grants. Other Bill Owens' titles with True North Editions include *The Village: Bill Owens' Jamaica, Bill Owens CARS: A Completely American Reality,* and *Bill Owens: The Legacy of Suburbia.*

Francesca Cosanti: I was born and grew up in Italy. I love to travel, not just with my mind, but to take inspiration from places, shapes, and colors. Currently, I work as an illustrator and a visual artist for publishing and advertising, collaborating with associations, companies, and agencies. My illustrations are realized mainly in digital with Mac or iPad. In my free time, I dedicate myself to my passions: dogs, food, swimming, books, travel, photography, and long walks.

Geir and Kate Jordahl bring their love of books and passion for images to the creation of a variety of visual projects. They founded True North Editions in 2012 as a collaborative effort to give voice to unique work by artists working authentically. They have worked together as a team since 1980 as editors, curators, and imagemakers. Geir and Kate Jordahl both have Masters of Fine Arts Degrees in Photography from Ohio University, Athens, Ohio. In 1983 they founded the PhotoCentral Program in Hayward, California, and were directors of PhotoCentral until 2020. Kate is a Professor Emerita of Photography at Foothill College, Los Altos Hills, California. The Jordahls now operate True North Editions based in Bellingham, Washington.

THE AMERICAN CARS COLORING BOOK

Created by Bill Owens
Illustrations by Francesca Cosanti
Designed by Kate Jordahl
Essay by Geir Jordahl

Copyright © 2025, Bill Owens Publishing
ISBN: 979-8-9860942-8-1

To order more copies, contact
bill@distilling.com

Billowens.com
Distilling.com
Delcoyears.com

www.ingramcontent.com/pod-product-compliance
Lightning Source LLC
Chambersburg PA
CBHW041541120626
46551CB00019B/2793